ABC Safari

An African Animal Adventure From A to Z

Written by Maria Moon

Copyright © 2025 by iloveloni
All rights reserved.

ISBN: 979-8-9932223-6-3

No part of this book may be reproduced, stored in a retrieval system, or transmitted in any form or by any means — electronic, mechanical, photocopying, recording, or otherwise — without prior written permission of the publisher, except for brief quotations used in reviews or articles.

For permissions, contact:
iloveloni
books@iloveloni.com

Written by Maria Moon

Design by iloveloni

Printed in the United States of America

iloveloni

www.iloveloni.com

My Lovely

Book

This book belongs to

Welcome to Africa!

Get ready for an amazing adventure! Africa is the second largest continent in the world, beautiful and full of wild animals, colorful birds, and exciting places to explore. One of those places is the Safari. Safari means a journey or expedition. On our ABC Safari we will meet a new animal for every letter of the alphabet - from A to Z!

Did you know that Africa is home to the "Big Five" animals – lion, leopard, elephant, buffalo and rhinoceros? You will get to see plenty of other animals that call Africa home as well. So, grab your Safari hat and your binoculars – our ABC Safari through Africa is about to begin!
Enjoy the fun safari activities included at the end!

Let the journey begin.

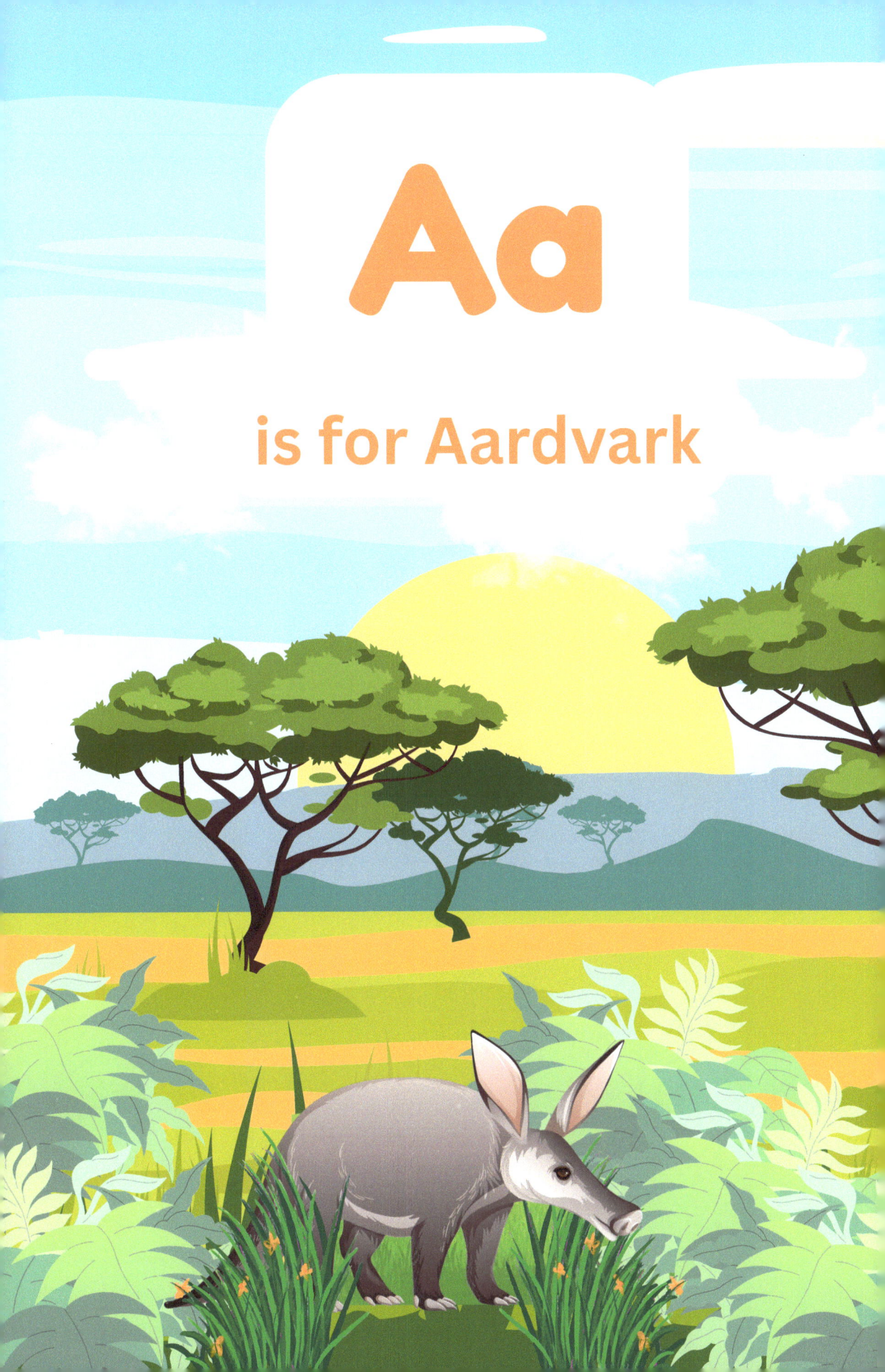

On my safari, what do I see? A Baboon looking at me.

On my safari, what do I see?
A Drongo looking at me.

On my safari, what do I see? A huge Elephant looking at me.

On my safari, what do I see? A long neck Giraffe looking at me.

On my safari, what do I see? A hungry Hippo looking at me.

On my safari, what do I see? A sacred Ibis looking at me.

Jj is for Jackal

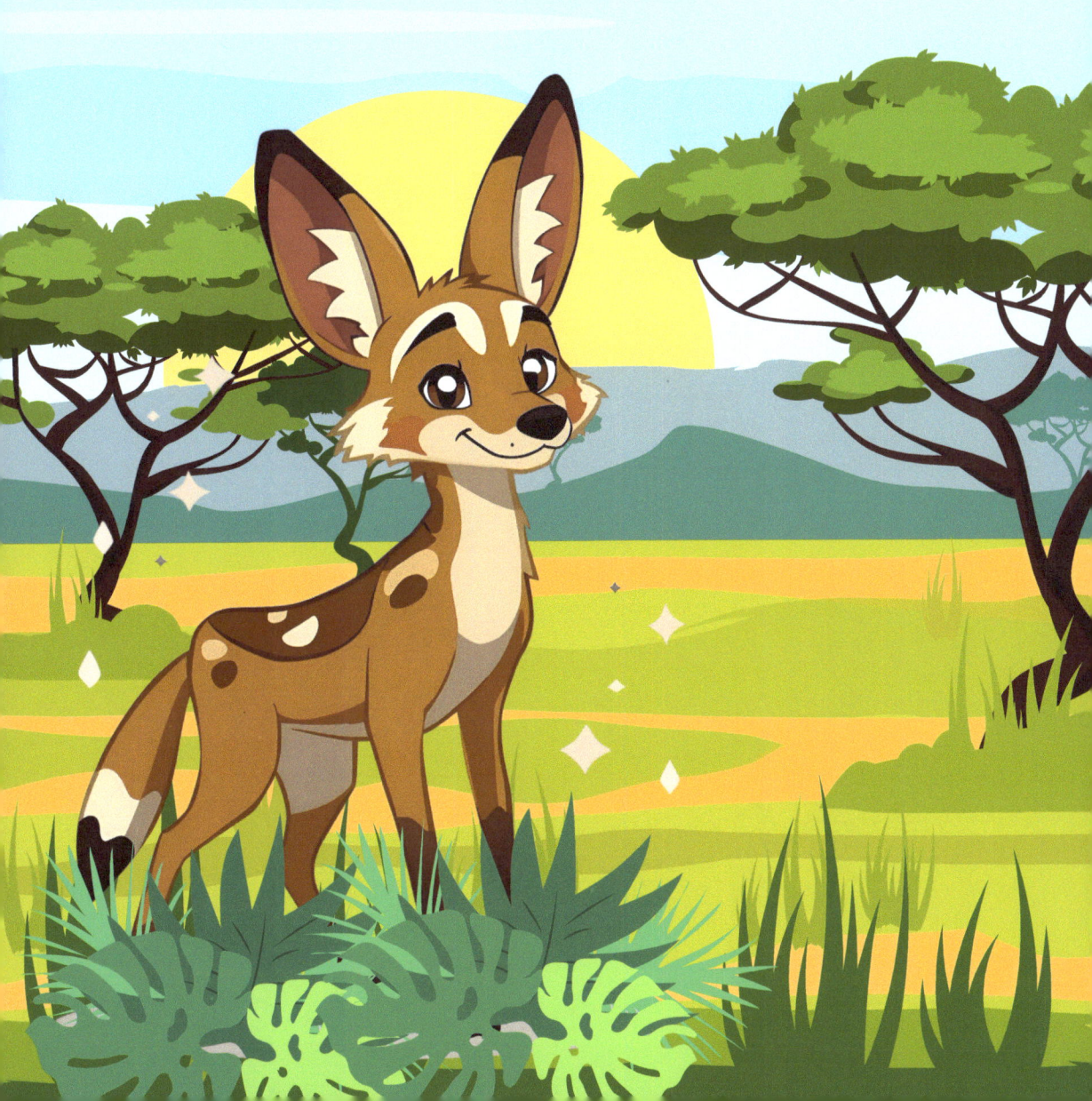

On my safari, what do I see? A Kori Bustard looking at me.

On my safari, what do I see? A brave Leopard looking at me.

On my safari, what do I see? A singing Nightingale looking at me.

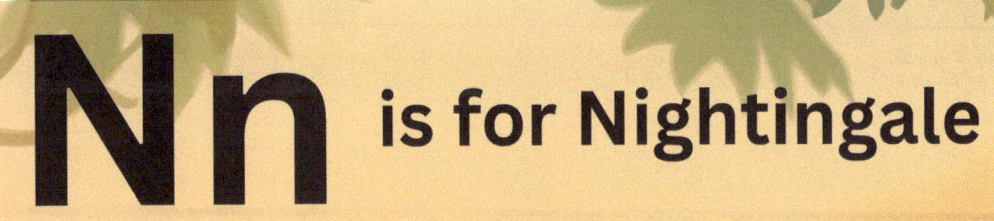

Nn is for Nightingale

On my safari, what do I see? An Ostrich looking at me.

On my safari, what do I see? A spikey Porcupine looking at me.

Pp is for Porcupine

On my safari, what do I see? A Quelea looking at me.

Qq is for Quelea

On my safari, what do I see? A huge Rhino looking at me.

Rr is for Rhinoceros

On my safari, what do I see? A slithering Snake looking at me.

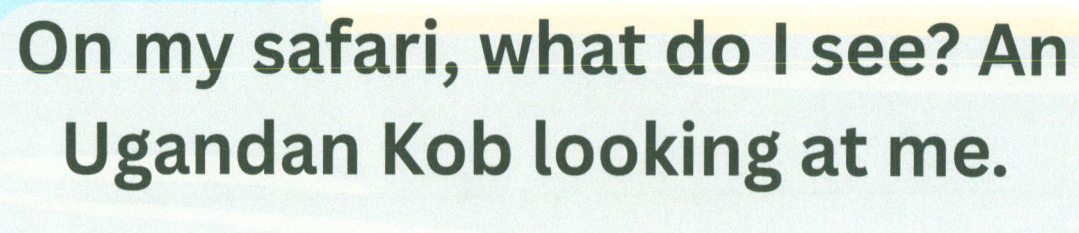
On my safari, what do I see? An Ugandan Kob looking at me.

Uu is for Ugandan Kob

On my safari, what do I see? A Vulture looking at me.

On my safari, what do I see? A Warthog looking at me.

Ww is for Warthog

On my safari, what do I see?
A Xerus looking at me.

On my safari, what do I see? A Yellow Mongoose looking at me.

Yy

is for Yellow Mongoose

On my safari, what do I see? A striped Zebra looking at me.

Safari Fun Zone

Which animal begins with an "L"?

Zebra

Giraffe

Leopard

Meerkat

Which animal starts with a "C"?

Snake

Ibis

Crocodile

Rhinoceros

Which animal start with a "V"?

Nightingale

Ostrich

Vulture

Which animal starts with a "J"?

Ugandan Kob

Jackal

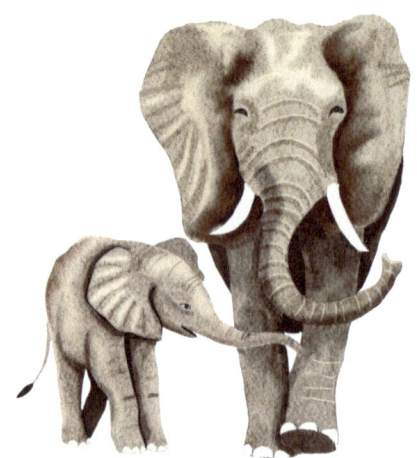

Elephant

Match the animal and letter to its name.

Match the animal and letter to its name.

 T

Giraffe

 Y

Tenrec

 G

Yellow Mongoose

Match the animal and letter to its name.

 R   Ugandan Kob

 A   Rhinoceros

 U   Aardvark

Match the animal and letter to its name.

   H   Meerkat

   M   Ostrich

   O

                    Hippopotamus

Help the Giraffe find her way back home.

MAZE #1

Get the plants to the hungry Zebra.

MAZE #2

Help the Meerkat get to the other side of the tunnel.

MAZE #3

Help the Leopard to the tree.

MAZE #4

Guess the shadow.

Guess the shadow.

Guess the shadow.

Guess the shadow.

Answer Page

Which animal begins with an "L"?

 Leopard

Which animal starts with a "C"?

 Crocodile

Which animal starts with a "V"?

 Vulture

Which animal starts with a "J"?

 Jackal

Match the animal and letter to its name.

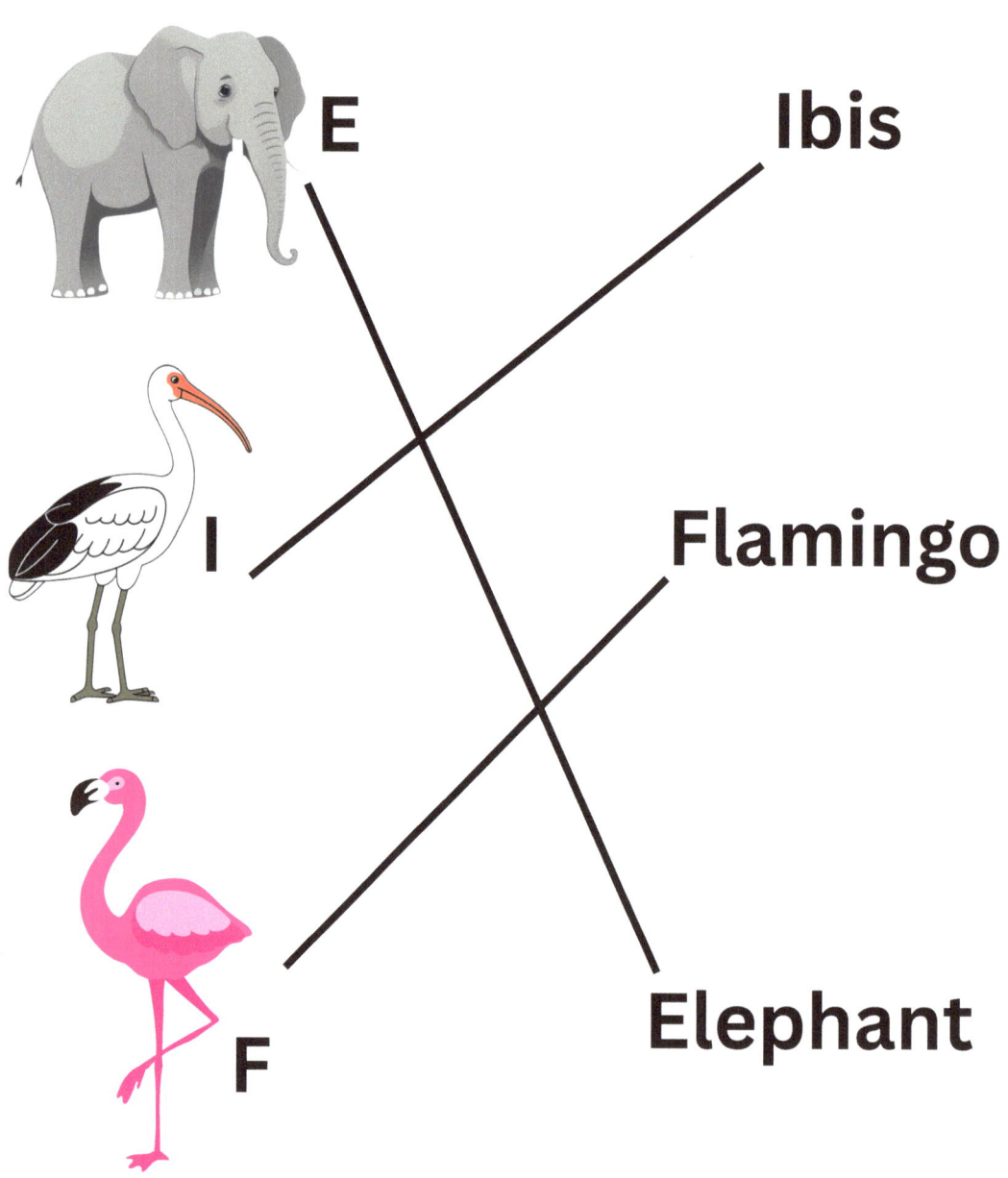

Match the animal and letter to its name.

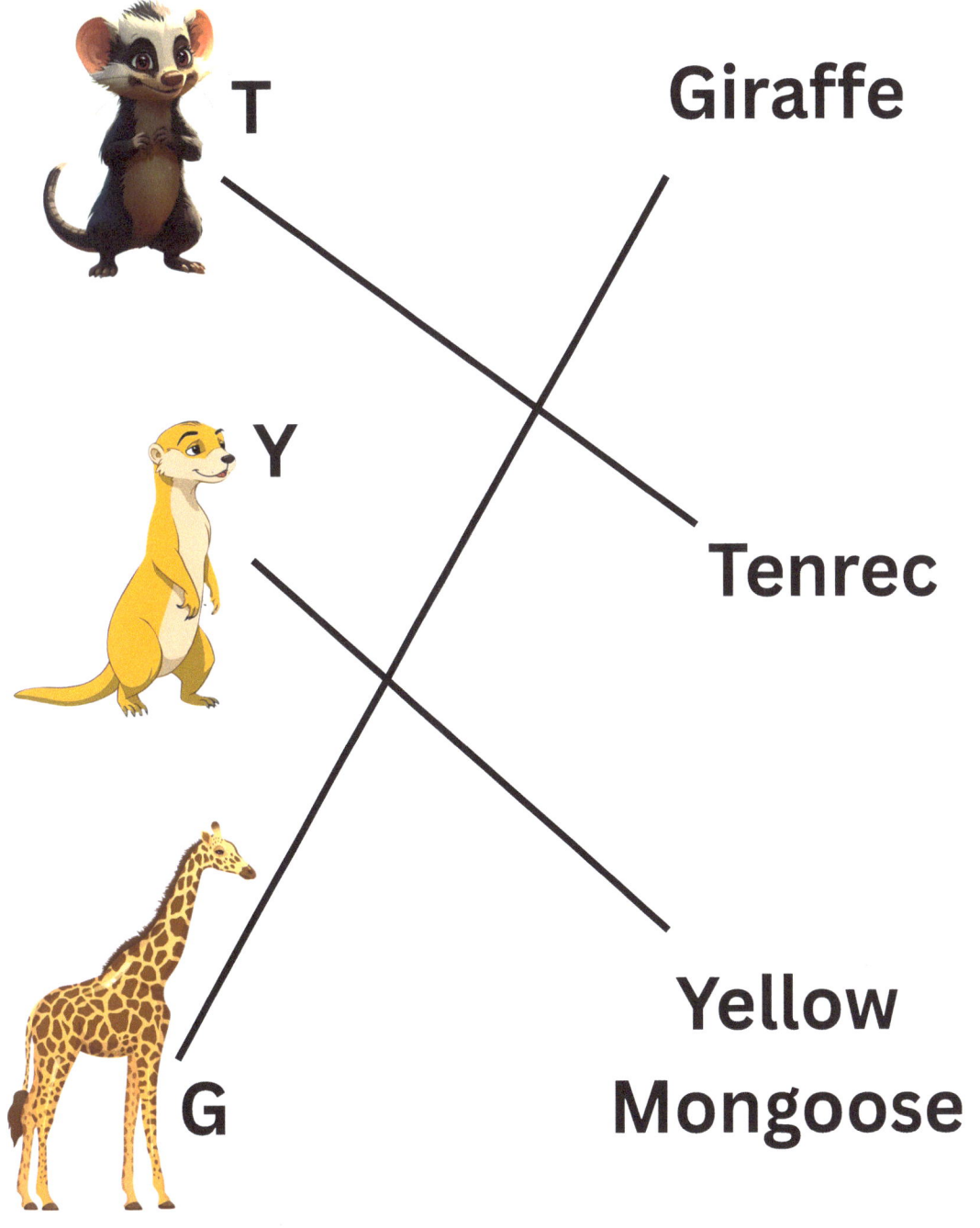

Match the animal and letter to its name.

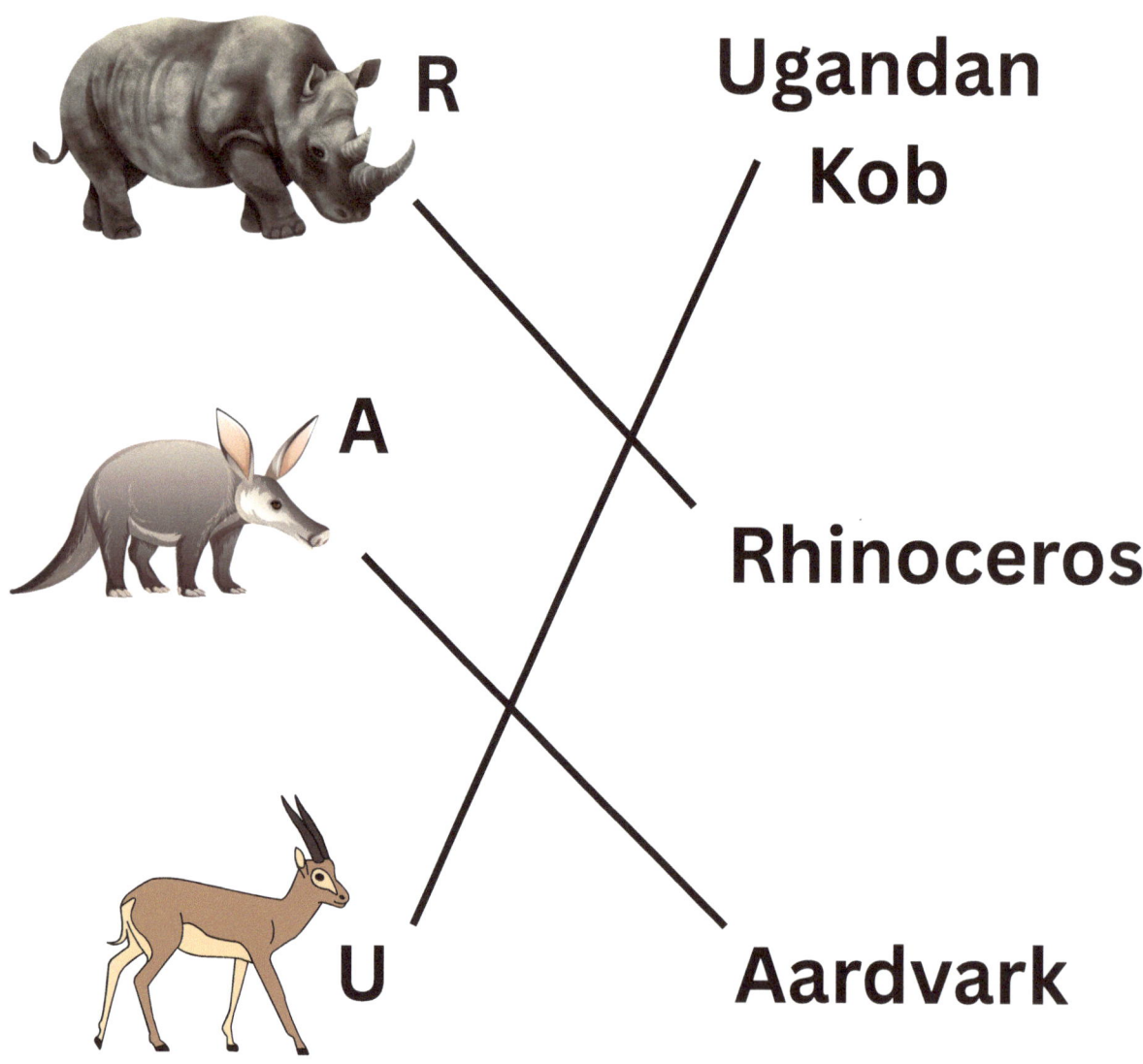

Match the animal and letter to its name.

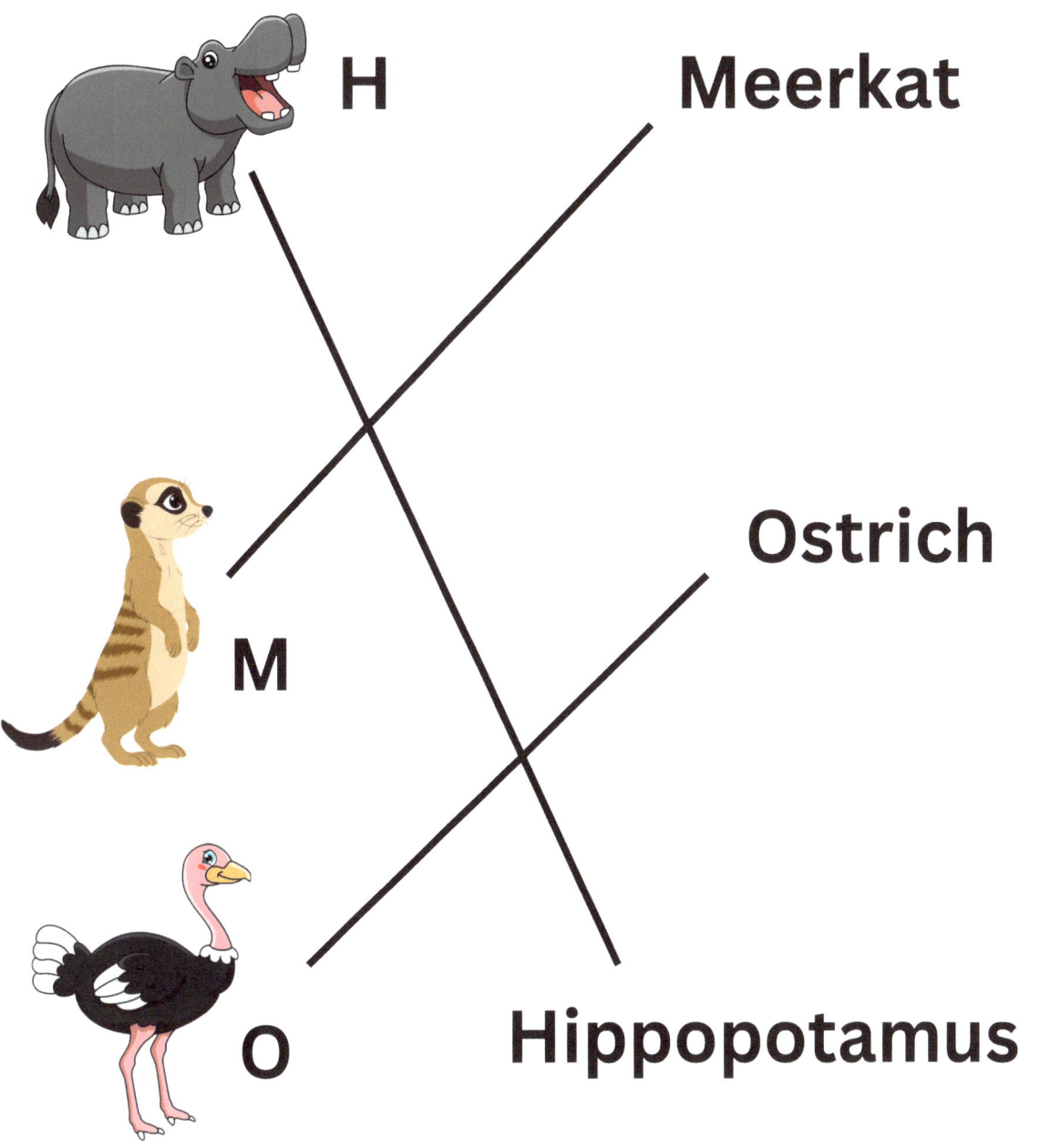

MAZE SOLUTION #1

MAZE SOLUTION #2

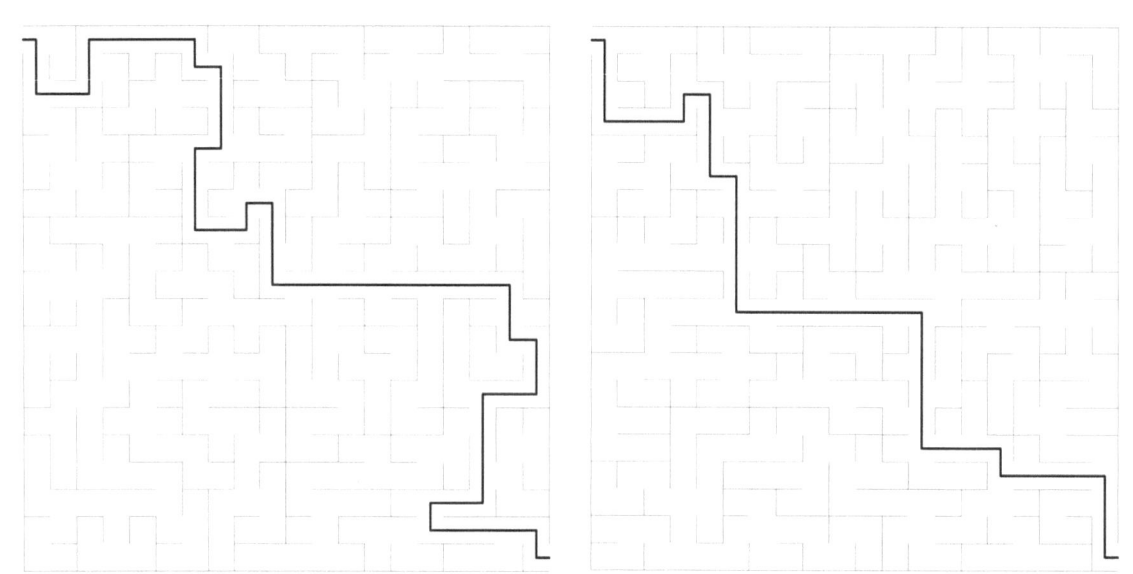

MAZE SOLUTION #3

MAZE SOLUTION #4

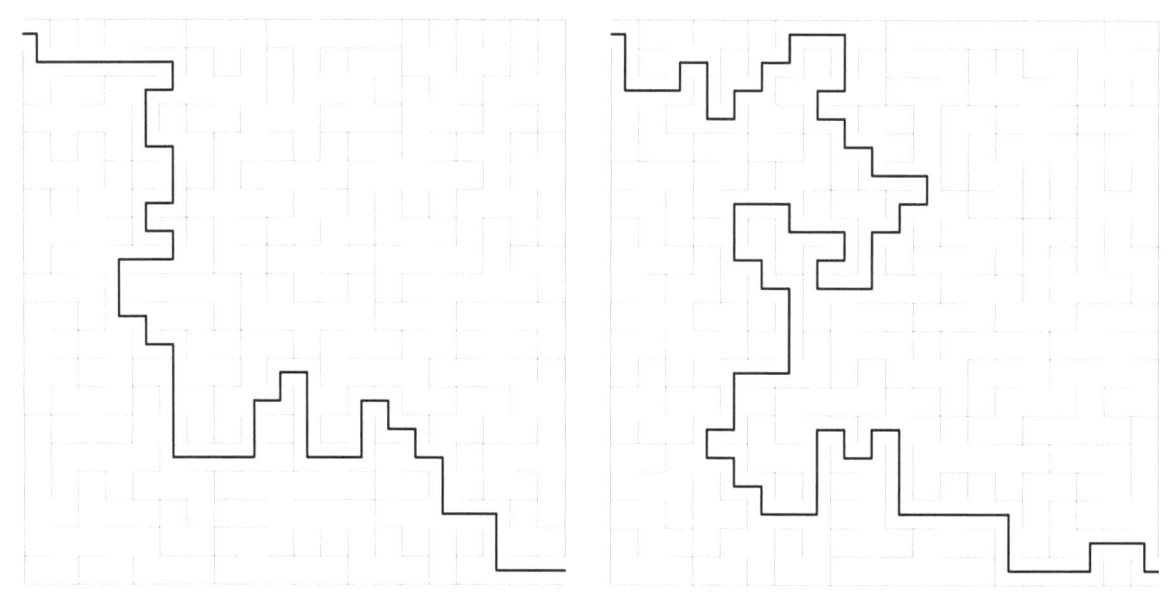

Elephant

Giraffe

Rhinoceros

Flamingo

www.ingramcontent.com/pod-product-compliance
Lightning Source LLC
Chambersburg PA
CBHW041136130526
44582CB00031B/139